❋ Influential Li

CHRISTINA AGUILERA

Pop Singer

Enslow Publishing
101 W. 23rd Street
Suite 240
New York, NY 10011
USA

enslow.com

Richard Worth

Published in 2016 by Enslow Publishing, LLC
101 W. 23rd Street, Suite 240, New York, NY 10011

Library of Congress Cataloging-in-Publication Data
Worth, Richard.
 Christina Aguilera: pop singer / Richard Worth.
    pages cm. — (Influential latinos)
 Includes bibliographical references and index.
 Summary: "Describes the life and successes of pop singer Christina Aguilera"— Provided by publisher.
 ISBN 978-0-7660-7180-3
 1. Aguilera, Christina, 1980—Juvenile literature. 2. Singers—United States—Biography—Juvenile literature. I. Title.
 ML3930.A36W67 2016
 782.42164092—dc23
 [B]
                              2015032636

Printed in the United States of America

To Our Readers: We have done our best to make sure all website addresses in this book were active and appropriate when we went to press. However, the author and the publisher have no control over and assume no liability for the material available on those websites or on any websites they may link to. Any comments or suggestions can be sent by e-mail to customerservice@enslow.com.

Photo Credits: Cover, p. 1 Helga Esteb/Shuttertock.com; p. 4 Ethan Miller/Getty Images North America/Getty Images for dcp; p. 6 Everett Collection; pp. 7, 34 Gregg DeGuire/WireImage/Getty Images; p. 9 Michael Tran/FilmMagic/Getty Images; p. 11 The LIFE Picture Collection/Getty Images; p. 16 © Buena Vista Television/ Courtesy: Everett Collection; p. 21 Bob Berg/Hulton Archive/ Getty Images; p. 25 Everett Collection; p. 27 Jeff Vespa/WireImage/Getty Images; p. 28 JEFF HAYNES/AFP/Getty Images; p. 31 Bill Greenblatt/Liaison/Hulton Archive/Getty Images; p. 37 Mark Weiss/WireImage/Getty Images; p. 40 Kevin Winter/Getty Images Entertainment/Getty Images; p. 44 Stephen Lovekin/Getty Images Entertainment/Getty Images for Montblanc; p. 47 Dimitrios Kambouris/WireImage/Getty Images; p. 48 Associated Press; p. 51 Kevin Kane/WireImage/Getty Images; p. 55 Kevin Mazur/WireImage for The Recording Academy/Getty Images; p. 59 Matthew Peyton/Getty Images Entertainment/Getty Images; p. 61 John Shearer/WireImage/Getty Images; p. 63 Harold Cunningham/WireImage/Getty Images; p. 66 Toby Canham/Getty Images Entertainment/Getty Images; p. 69 Bryan Bedder/DCP/Getty Images Entertainment/Getty Images for DCP; p. 72 Michael Caulfield/WireImage/Getty Images; p. 76 Donna Ward/Getty Images Entertainment/Getty Images; p. 79 © AF archive / Alamy Stock Photo; p. 82 © AF archive / Alamy Stock Photo; p. 89Joe Robbins/Getty Images Sport/Getty Images; p. 90 Lester Cohen/Wireimage/Getty Images; p. 94 Ethan Miller/Getty Images Entertainment/Getty Images; p. 96 Jason Merritt/Getty Images Entertainment/Getty Images; p. 99 Frederick M. Brown/Getty Images Entertainment/Getty Images; p. 102 Kevin Winter/Hulton Archive/Getty Images; p. 105 Tim Roney/Hulton Archive/Getty Images; p. 110 Gregg DeGuire/WireImage/Getty Images.

Contents

Christina Aguilera performs at the 50th Academy of Country Music Awards in 2015.

Chapter 1

A CHILD STAR

"Good Evening. Welcome to *Star Search*," began Ed McMahon, the smiling host of the popular television talent show. *Star Search* was a highly successful program that ran for thirteen seasons, from 1983 to 1995. The show introduced talented young artists in a variety of categories, including male and female vocalist, junior vocalist, teen dance, vocal group, and comedy. Each week two contestants competed in each category in front of a panel of four judges. One of the contestants was selected as the champion and the other as the challenger.

Star Search became the first stop for a variety of talented young people who began successful careers. Beyoncé appeared on the show in 1993 in the female vocalist category, and that same year Justin Timberlake appeared in the competition for best male vocalist.

Britney Spears appeared when she was only eleven years old as a junior vocalist. She was beaten by twelve-year-old Marty Thomas. Although Thomas had a career on television and on stage in New York City, it was nowhere near as big as Spears' success. As a competitor on *Star Search*, you did not need to win to become famous.

Star Search was a popular television talent show hosted by Ed McMahon that ran from 1983 to 1995.

Justin Timberlake, who was known as Justin Randall at the time he appeared on the program, sang in a country music style. But he wasn't quite good enough to become the champion in his category. Instead, he was beaten by Anna Nardona. She later became a preschool teacher, while Timberlake went on to fame and fortune. In fact, several people who were runner-ups did far better than the champions.[1]

In 1990, a nine-year-old girl appeared on *Star Search* in the junior vocalist category. Although she was small, she had a huge voice. Gripping the microphone in her hand, she belted out "The Greatest Love of All," a hit sung by popular singer Whitney Houston. Unfortunately, the little girl wasn't quite good enough to win.

"I was a good sport about it," she recalled. "My Mom made me go back out and shake [the winner's] hand and tell him I was happy he won. Tears were running down my face. Awful."[2]

Almost no one remembers the name of the winner in the junior vocalist category on that *Star Search* episode. But the runner-up would later become famous. Her name was Christina Aguilera.

Christina Aguilera has been in the public eye since she was nine years old, when she made it to the semifinals in *Star Search*.

Chapter 2

A YOUNG SINGING SENSATION

"**P**ractically since I was out of diapers I wanted to become a singer," Christina Aguilera once said. "I mean, this is my ultimate love. Ever since I've been out of diapers, I've loved to sing."[1] Why did Christina have such an overwhelming desire for a singing career? As with many people, Christina's success arose from a complex set of motives.

Christina Aguilera was born on December 18, 1980, in Staten Island, New York. Staten Island is one of the five boroughs—parts—of New York City. Her parents, Shelly Loraine Fidler and Fausto Wagner Xavier Aguilera, had only been married for a short time before Christina was born.

Christina's father, Fausto Aguilera, had lived in poverty in Guayaquil, Ecuador. At nineteen, he had immigrated with the rest of his family to Staten Island. The Aguilera family had come to the United States hoping to escape oppressive economic conditions in Ecuador for a better life in America. Many immigrants had come before them, looking for exactly the same thing.

Fausto eventually enlisted in the Army. It provided training, steady employment, and the opportunity to earn a much better income than he could ever have made in Ecuador. He also had a chance to travel and visit some other parts of the world.

At age thirty-one, Fausto met Shelly Fidler. She was only nineteen years old. Shelly was a talented musician who played both violin and piano. Her mother, Delcie Fidler, persuaded her at the age of sixteen to play with the Youth Symphony Orchestra on their grand tour of Europe. When she grew older, Shelly attended college, where she was studying to be a Spanish translator. Her fluency in Spanish may have been one of the reasons that she attracted Fausto Aguilera. She also had a deep interest

Christina's mother, Shelly, was a talented musician in her own right. Throughout Christina's childhood, she continued to support her daughter's dreams, booking auditions and performances.

in Spanish culture, which was no doubt appealing to the young man.

After their marriage, Fausto was transferred by the Army to Staten Island. Following Christina's birth, the Army continued to move the family to a variety of different posts in the United States and abroad. These included Texas, New Jersey, and Sagamihara, Japan. Christina never had one home or one school, and she had very little opportunity to make any friends. Meanwhile, Shelly's life with Fausto had grown increasingly unhappy. The couple seemed to argue regularly, and Fausto physically abused his wife. Christina not only heard the brutal arguments, but also witnessed some of the beatings that her mother received.

Shelly left Fausto on several occasions, taking Christina with her. But she always returned, possibly because she still loved Fausto. Finally, after the US Army moved them back from Japan, to a base near Philadelphia, Shelly left Fausto for good. With Christina, age six, and a baby named Rachel, Shelly moved in with her mother in a suburb outside of Pittsburgh, Pennsylvania.

A Singer Is Born

Christina had inherited some of her mother's musical talent. While the conflicts between her parents became more and more brutal, Christina tried to hide from the constant unpleasantness in music. "I would seriously run up to my bedroom and put on that *Sound of Music* tape. Julie Andrews [the star of the 1965 film and a gifted singer] was free and alive and she was playful and rebellious. . . .I know it sounds really cheesy, but that was my escape. I would open my bedroom and window and I would just imagine the audience. I would just sing out."[2]

Christina went to music stores looking for records of her favorite singers—jazz vocalists Etta James and Billie Holiday. She performed in her room in front of a collection of stuffed animals. After she memorized and practiced a song, she would also perform in front of her grandmother. Delcie recognized that Christina had

As a young girl, Christina had mature taste in music. While many girls her age favored pop music, she gravitated toward the jazz greats.

real talent, just as she had spotted the natural gifts that Shelly had for music. And Delcie persuaded Christina to perform at neighborhood parties and in record stores.

As Christina put it, "I was known around town as the little girl with the big voice. Once, when I was seven, this guy couldn't believe I was singing, so he unplugged my microphone in the middle of my song, which freaked me out. Then he was like, 'Oh my gosh, she's really singing!'"[3]

At this time, *Star Search* had already become a popular show on television. So Christina's family sent an audition tape to *Star Search,* which payed her expenses to Hollywood and guaranteed Christina $1,000 no matter how well she did on the show. Although she lost, Christina's performance led to a long article about her in a local Pittsburgh newspaper, which praised the singing voice of the local girl who had appeared on *Star Search.*

Meanwhile, Jude Pohl, a Pittsburgh music producer, had heard about Christina. After seeing her audition tape, Pohl wanted to book Christina on his own local version of *Star Search.* "It wasn't that she had a big voice," he said. "She had an *adult* voice."[4] And Pohl booked her on his show.

Christina was gradually becoming a local celebrity, but it was a mixed blessing. While each appearance brought her closer to a singing career, it brought her no new friends at school. Shelly recalled that the other girls were jealous of Christina and even bullied her. The situation had become so bad that Christina was afraid to go to school.

One of Christina's teachers tried to help. "She was just so much better than everybody else—head and shoulders above everybody," explained Penny Householder. "They were just, you know, normal children. And she [in contrast] had this wonderful talent." A friend, Marcie Craig Reilly explained that Christina was regularly being taunted by her classmates. "I remember one time in gym class they were trying to kick balls at her, deliberately trying to hurt her. It was just a jealousy thing."[5]

And it was not only Christina who suffered. "As soon as *Star Search* happened," she recalled, "a lot of my mom's old friends, other parents, wouldn't talk to us anymore."[6] They may have been jealous or just convinced that it was inappropriate for a mother to promote her young daughter on a popular television show for the rest of America to see.

When Christina was only nine, her mother spotted an advertisement in a Pittsburgh newspaper for girls and boys to audition for *The All New Mickey Mouse Club*. Shelly took her daughter to the local tryouts, and Christina performed better than most of the 400 other children. Although she was good, the producers decided that Christina was too young to be on the show.

But Shelly didn't give up. Two years later, in 1991, Christina was performing at a large dinner in Pittsburgh. After her appearance, she was asked by the Pittsburgh Steelers of the National Football League and the Pittsburgh Penguins of the National Hockey League to sing the National Anthem at their local games. This

The Mickey Mouse Club

The original *Mickey Mouse Club* television show began appearing in the United States during the 1950s. It starred everyone's favorite cartoon mouse, Mickey Mouse, who was accompanied by a group of real, live young people, who sang and danced.

In addition, the daily program featured Disney cartoons, stories about the Hardy Boys (a popular detective book series), and guest stars. Each day also had a different theme, such as "Fun With Music Day" on Mondays; "Guest Star Day" on Tuesdays; and "Anything Can Happen Day" on Wednesdays.

Every show opened with the same theme song: "Who's the leader of the club that's made for you and me? M-I-C-K-E-Y M-O-U-S-E." The show was revised in the 1970s and again in the late 1980s, when it was called *The New Mickey Mouse Club* and *The All New Mickey Mouse Club*.

not only gave her a chance to perform, but to perform in front of large crowds. "I was the youngest anthem singer ever, for a while," Christina recalled. "I became a huge hockey fan."[7] And she clearly loved the experience.

Then a big break occurred for Christina. The producers of *The All New Mickey Mouse Club* re-discovered the tape she had made three years earlier. At twelve, they were ready to reconsider her, considering Christina old enough now to appear on the show. Along with 15,000 other boys and girls she tried out for one of seven spots on the show. And this time, she made it, joining two other people who would eventually become stars, Britney Spears and Justin Timberlake.

Chapter 3

CHRISTINA'S GROWING FAMILY

In 1992, Christina's world changed in two very important ways. The first change came when her mother, Shelly, married again. Shelly's husband—and Christina's new stepfather—was Jim Kearns, a paramedic with two children. A sensitive, caring man, Kearns gave Christina's life a new sense of stability. And his two children—Casey, seven, and Stephanie, four—doubled the size of her family.

But the most profound change may have been the large, extended family she joined in Orlando, Florida—the home of *The All New Mickey Mouse Club*. Christina, Shelly, and the rest of the family moved into an apartment building that had been reserved for the show's cast, the Mouseketeers. Episodes of *The All New Mickey Mouse Club* were taped from May to October each year. After taping ended the family moved back to Pittsburgh.

Christina was part of a talented cast in *The All New Mickey Mouse Club*, including Britney Spears, Justin Timberlake, and Ryan Gosling.

Mouseketeers ranged in age from eleven to eighteen. Christina bonded with one of the younger girls—Britney Spears. Shelly and Britney's mother, Lynne, also became very close friends. The girls "would even study together, with three hours per day of compulsory schooling part of the Disney contract," according to author Chloe Govan. "Christina was a perfectionist, maintaining a straight-A average and fascinated by English and science."[1]

The All New Mickey Mouse Club ran every weekday after school, at 5:30 in the afternoon. Christina, Britney, and other Mouseketeers performed in song and dance numbers as well as comedy skits. On one show, the guest star was singer Whitney Houston. Houston was a pop star with one of history's biggest voices, and she was one of one of Christina's idols. Christina wanted to develop a style similar to Houston's for singing pop songs and blues. "They called me Little Diva on that show, or Mini-Diva," Christina recalled. "Because I had a little strut."[2]

Appearing on *The All New Mickey Mouse Club* was not enough to make Christina Aguilera famous. Nor was it any guarantee of future success. But a starring role at age twelve was certainly an important step forward in a young girl's career.

Christina seemed happy to be working with other girls her age who also shared her ambitions and wanted to become singing stars. She knew that her own goals were not unique or unusual. Unfortunately her experience in Orlando was quite different from what she found after the taping ended, when she returned to school in

Pennsylvania. There, some of the students still made fun of Christina and tried to avoid her. Some even bullied her. While it wasn't easy for her to accept this treatment, now at least she knew that for almost half the year she could live in Orlando among other young people just like herself.

Big Breaks

While performing in Florida, Christina met publicity agent Ruth Inniss. Inniss was associated with RCA Records, a well-known recording company. One day, she

Whitney Houston (1963–2012)

Born in Newark, New Jersey, Whitney Houston became one of the best-selling recording artists in the history of pop music. Her first album, *Whitney Houston*, recorded in 1985, was named best album of 1986 by *Rolling Stone* magazine. In 1992, she starred in the film *The Bodyguard*, which featured her hit song, "I Will Always Love You." This song had been written in 1973 by country artist Dolly Parton, but flew largely under the radar until Houston recorded it. "I Will Always Love You" became the top-selling record ever released by a woman vocalist. Houston also recorded the music for the film, *The Preacher's Wife* in 1996, which became gospel music's highest-selling soundtrack.

Houston received numerous Grammy Awards—awards given annually to outstanding vocalists, musicians, and songwriters. Tragically, she was troubled by drug addiction and drowned in a hotel bathtub in 2012.

heard Christina perform and afterward told Shelly that she might be able to help the young Mouseketeer with a singing career. At that point, Christina was absorbed with taping episodes of the show, and also making contracted appearances at Disneyworld in Orlando. There she signed autographs for children visiting the park who recognized her from *The All New Mickey Mouse Club.*

But in 1994, Shelly agreed that Ruth Inniss should become Christina's manager and guide her career. Shelly recognized, if no one else did, that the show would not go on indefinitely, and Christina needed to begin planning for the next stage of her career. For that to happen, an experienced agent was essential.

In fact, the final season of *The All New Mickey Mouse Club* appeared on television in 1995, after being recorded the previous year. By this time, Christina was moving into the next phase of her career under the guidance of Ruth Inniss. In New Jersey, Inniss connected Christina with two music producers—Robert Alleca and Michael Brown—whom Inniss had worked with in Florida. They suggested that Christina come into their studio to record an album that might be sent to recording companies.

In 1995, she recorded twelve songs for an album that would be titled *Just Be Free.* She sang the title song in both English and Spanish. All the songs were co-written by Christina. *Just Be Free* was designed as a "demo" album, one to be sent to recording companies who might consider hiring Christina, based on her performances.

Unfortunately, no company was impressed enough to work with Christina. Nevertheless, she did succeed in going on tour to Brasov, Romania, and Tokyo, Japan. There she recorded with Keizo Nakanishi, one of Japan's leading pop recording stars, a song called "All I Wanna Do." Unfortunately, however, this song never became a hit.

According to Christina, "My dream [had] always been to record an album before I was out of high school."[3] Since she wasn't yet finished with high school, Christina still had several years in which to realize her dream.

Meanwhile, one of Christina's demo tapes had found its way to Ron Fair, who worked for RCA Records. One of the songs was Whitney Houston's "Run to You," which so impressed Fair that he called Christina to the RCA studios. By this time, Ruth Inniss was co-managing Christina with Normand Kurtz, a successful music lawyer. However, Kurtz decided to take Christina's career out of Inniss's hands and put his son, Steve Kurtz, in charge of her.

It was a very high-handed move for Kurtz to do this. But neither Shelly nor Christina stopped him. And the Kurtz father-and-son team had far more experience and better connections in the music business than Ruth Inniss could provide for Christina. If they wanted to reach the next level, they had to move beyond Inniss.

Steve and Normand Kurtz presented Christina to Ron Fair, who recalled: "[S]he basically got into that performance zone and sang. . .with a complete sense of self-possession, with perfect intonation. She was very

It may be difficult to believe today, but at first, Christina couldn't find a record company interested in working with her.

determined and extremely professional. . . . I went to my boss and said, 'This girl's the bomb, let's sign her!'"[4] And with that, Christina Aguilera was signed to a contract with RCA Records.

Soon afterward, Fair was contacted by Disney studios for someone to sing the theme song, "Reflection," for a new animated film titled *Mulan*. The song was difficult because it required the singer to hit an especially high note right after a note in the middle range. But Christina was convinced that she had the ability to sing the notes.

"To prove that she could do it," the *Pittsburgh-Post Gazette* reported, "she grabbed a cheap tape recorder, recorded a song with the note they wanted at full strength and sent off the tape. Disney flew her to Los Angeles."[5]

Once there, Christina was given singing lessons to sharpen and refine her voice. Then she spent the next five days recording various takes of "Reflection" until everyone was completely satisfied. Disney also arranged to have Christina star in her first music video, featuring the song. Christina stayed in Los Angeles to hear her rendition of the song backed by a full orchestra. "It's enough to bring tears to your eyes to hear a 90-piece orchestra playing your song. It was amazing."[6] By July 1998, shortly after the song's release, it was a number one hit across America. And Christina Aguilera was about to become very famous.

Chapter 4

TEEN POP STAR

In September 1999, the *Washington Post* reporter, Richard Harrington, compared Christina Aguilera to other pop singing sensations, like Britney Spears, who had appeared on *The All New Mickey Mouse Club*. "Of those, Aguilera would seem to have the most musical potential, thanks to a genuinely powerful voice that evoked comparisons to the younger Mariah Carey and Whitney Houston."[1]

After Christina's success with "Reflection," RCA had spent about $1 million on production and voice lessons to turn her into the newest pop star. In June 1999, this had led to the release of a new single, "Genie in a Bottle." A leading American music magazine, *Billboard,* rapidly moved it to its Hot 100 list of top singles and after only three weeks it was among the top five on the list. Soon it reached number one and stayed there for five weeks—an incredible achievement for a young, nearly unknown young singer.[2]

RCA had spent a great deal of money promoting the single. Its publicity agents went on the Internet, mentioning the single on message boards as well as websites that were popular with teens. Christina's mother ran her daughter's new website, answering questions from her fans, and publicizing the new music video that soon accompanied the hit record.

However, "Genie in a Bottle" also came in for a significant amount of criticism for some of its lyrics, which seemed sexually suggestive. In one line, Christina sings: "My body's saying let's go, but my heart is saying no." Christina pointed out that this line simply reflected the moral struggle that many teenagers experience during adolescence. While the song's lyrics may have reflected what some teens wanted to hear, their parents were not so happy with the choice of words.

Nevertheless, this issue did not prevent her from making a guest appearance on the *Tonight Show* with Jay Leno or on a Christmas Show in the White House with President Bill Clinton. In addition, Aguilera made appearances at the American Music Awards, the Super Bowl half-time show in 2000, and *Total Request Live* on MTV. For RCA, she had become a hot property, and the record company was doing everything possible to promote her and increase the sales of her recordings. RCA executive Jack Rovner said, "I've worked with Mariah [and] Whitney. . .and Christina is in that league."[3]

Christina's First Album

RCA followed up on the success of the single "Genie in a Bottle," with the release of Christina's first album, simply titled *Christina Aguilera,* in 1999. The record company had assembled a team of writers and producers to achieve a pop sound. And, although Christina delivered it on the album, she said this was not always what she wanted to accomplish. "I was held back a lot from doing more R&B (Rhythm and Blues). They clearly wanted to make a fresh-sounding young pop record and that's not always the direction I wanted to go in. Sometimes they didn't get it, didn't want to hear me out because of my age, and that was a little bit frustrating."[4]

One of Christina's big breaks was performing as herself in a scene on the popular television show *Beverly Hills, 90210*.

The album included songs like, "Blessed," "Angel of Mine," "Love Will Find a Way," and "What a Girl Wants," which was a big hit.

Once again, RCA's publicity operation went into high gear, sending the talented Christina Aguilera and her first album to number one in America by the end of the year. By the beginning of 2000, "What a Girl Wants" had become the top-selling single recording in the United States. Finally at the Grammy Awards, Christina won the Grammy for the Best New Artist of 2000.

Meanwhile, Christina went on tour to Boston, San Francisco and Los Angeles, appearing in a duet with singer Enrique Iglesias at the 2000 Super Bowl, and in a concert in New York City. As it turned out, the

Stardom and Publicity

One of Christina's strongest motives to work hard and have hit singles was the publicity she received. The singer enjoyed signing autographs and appearing on popular shows like *Total Request Live*. First broadcast in 1998, this show aired music videos that were requested by its viewers who sent in their requests online. The show also featured guests like Britney Spears.

Although at first, Christina seemed almost overwhelmed by the amount of publicity she was receiving, the singer quickly grew accustomed to it. On a visit to Chicago, in fact, she was quite annoyed when an employee in the hotel where she was staying did not recognize her. As Christina put it, "He asked if I was [there] on vacation." She answered with impatience, "I only have the No. 1 single in the country."[5]

concert was attended by her father, Fausto, who had broken off contact with Christina twelve years earlier. Beginning at the concert, father and daughter began to reconnect. "There's always room for forgiveness, he's a part of my life now," she said. "It has been interesting getting reacquainted with my father."[6]

Although Christina was a star, she was also a nineteen-year-old teenager—one who wanted to have a good time. She was photographed at nightclubs with Iglesias and the host of *Total Request Live,* Carson Daly. She also admitted to having a crush on the rap star, Eminem. When Christina later said that she really had no interest in Eminem, especially because he was married, the rap star wrote a song with lyrics that claimed to describe intimate details of Christina's life. As *Rolling Stone* magazine put it, "it is probably the worst thing that could happen to a nineteen-year-old ... like high school all over again."[7]

While Christina may have had a star's voice, she was showing

All of Christina's ambition and hard work paid off when she won the Grammy Award for the Best New Artist of 2000.

Another highlight of the year 2000 came in January, when Christina performed "Celebrate the Future Hand in Hand" with fellow Latino and pop superstar Enrique Iglesias during the half-time show of Super Bowl XXXIV.

herself to be very naïve. She had not yet learned that her every statement had become news for newspaper articles and popular magazines. And her every appearance—no matter where and no matter with whom—attracted a crowd of photographers just waiting for a shot of her.

As she told the *Rolling Stone* reporter, "I've been on my own, and it's kind of lonely and crazy when so much stuff is thrown at you. Sometimes you feel like the whole world is waiting for you to mess up."[8] Christina was beginning to grow up very fast and become aware that stardom—which she had dreamed about for so long—had a positive and a negative side.

Chapter 5

LOVE AND SUCCESS

In summer 2000, Christina began her first solo tour. It was sponsored by Levi's, the jeans manufacturer, and Sears, the large department store chain. In fact, to appeal to younger shoppers, Sears had already opened a chain of 650 Christina Aguilera boutiques in their stores. They featured Christina's CDs and her T-shirts.[1] In Milwaukee, Wisconsin, where the tour opened, she told a crowd of 17,000 fans, "You guys, this is my first headlining tour!"[2]

She sang songs from her best-selling album accompanied by her band and her dancers. Unknown to her millions of fans, one of them had become very special to her. Christina later told a reporter that she had fallen in love with Jorge Santos. When she moved from New York to Los Angeles, Jorge also moved to his own apartment there to be closer to her.

After playing Milwaukee, the tour went north to Canada, appearing in Ottawa and Winnipeg. During the tour, Christina also checked into recording studios where she was working on a new, Spanish-language album, titled *Mi Reflejo* (My Reflection). Although Christina understood Spanish, she did not speak it well. As a result, she had to take Spanish lessons before recording the songs.

The album featured songs such as "Falsas Esperanzas" (False Hopes), "Si No Te Hubiera Conocido" (If I Hadn't Known You), as well as a duet with Puerto Rican singer, Luis Fonsi. Once the album was released in September, it became number one in Latin America for twenty weeks.

Capitalizing on her success, Christina was also working on an album of Christmas songs. It included her rendition of "Silent Night," and one of her favorites, "Climb Every Mountain," from the film *The Sound of Music*, which had inspired her as a child. Between the tour and the recordings, the pace was exhausting, and Christina almost collapsed from the effort.

But hard work, Christina believed, would pay off. One of her biographers explained: "Her concern was that she would be seen as a shallow, superficial fantasy image. Inevitably such a career would be a transitory one as looks faded with age—and besides, she felt she had far more to offer than mere surface appeal."[3] She had no intention of being a "flash in the pan," popular today like many pop stars, and gone tomorrow. She intended to last, and with her powerful voice, Christina had the ability to enjoy many years of success. But it took almost continuous hard work, which left her with very little

At the same time she embarked on her first solo tour, beginning in the summer of 2000, Christina recorded a Spanish-language album.

time for her relationship with Jorge Santos. As a result, their relationship began to feel the negative effects of her nonstop schedule.

"She never stops and she is always so afraid to disappoint her fans," Shelly explained. "I've seen her sick literally from exhaustion on more than one occasion even when I, and others, have asked her to cancel so she can rest—but she always said the people might be disappointed."[4]

But, whether Christina realized it or not, she had already begun disappointing her fans. During her tour, she seemed to have very little time to speak to teenagers or sign autographs, even after her fans had waited hours to see her. In July, when her group played in Pittsburgh, the *Post-Gazette* reported, "Earlier that day, a crowd of 30. . .stood waiting outside Aguilera's swanky downtown hotel, many clutching *Rolling Stone.* . .with the singer on the cover. When she finally emerged, a knapsack hanging off her back, a bodyguard hustled her onto the tour bus in the time it took to scribble maybe six or seven autographs. . . ."[5]

That same article addressed Christina's place in the increasingly crowded field of young pop starlets, such as Britney Spears, Jessica Simpson, and Mandy Moore. "What separates the *Genie* [Christina] from other pop stars of the moment is the voice," wrote reporter Ed Masley in the *Post-Gazette*, "an awe-inspiring instrument she uses like a girl who spent her childhood dreaming she could one day be the next Mariah Carey. And today, of course, she is."[6]

Mariah Carey

Mariah Carey, one of Christina Aguilera's role models and idols, is about ten years older than Aguilera. She shot to stardom with her album *Mariah Carey,* released in 1990, which became an immediate hit and led to a series of singles, each of them reaching number one on the *Billboard* Hot 100 chart. Three more successful albums followed in the 1990s, including *Emotions, Music Box,* and *Daydream.*

The World Music Awards later named Carey the world's top-selling singer of the 1990s. Early in the next decade, Carey's life turned downward as she suffered a breakdown. But this was followed by a return to stardom with the release of *The Emancipation of Mimi* in 2005. One of its songs, "We Belong Together," later became the "Song of the Decade" according to *Billboard* magazine. Carey has also won numerous Grammy Awards, World Music Awards, and American Music Awards. Her powerful voice and effective song styling as a pop and R&B singer enabled her blaze a path for Christina Aguilera and other singers to follow.

A New Direction

In an effort to change her image and ensure her continuing success, Christina believed that the time had come to move in a new direction. Her manager, Steve Kurtz, had been very instrumental in Christina's success with the first three albums. But Christina worried that she was known primarily as a blonde teeny-bopper, and every time she expressed a desire to change her image or

Christina dreamed of being the next Mariah Carey. Although the two divas have carved their own niches, both have big, lush voices.

sing with a different style, she had met strong opposition from Kurtz.

Finally, in October 2000, she filed a lawsuit against Kurtz, claiming that he had not properly managed her career. Kurtz, of course, disagreed, saying that he had enabled Christina to achieve financial success. But Christina was eager to set off in a new direction, one that would help her continue to retain her stardom for decades to come. She did not want fans to see her as just another "dumb blonde" and talked about dying her hair black. This was part of her desire to create a different image. In addition, she wanted to add more of an R&B sound to her music, much like her role model, Mariah Carey.

What's more, she felt that Kurtz's management of her career had led her to the point of complete exhaustion. While on tour, Christina had been stopping at local studios to work on her new albums, *Mi Reflejo* and *My Kind of Christmas*. It was far too much for Christina, and she wanted her life to change.

Eventually, the case was settled, and Christina took on a new manager, Irving Azoff. She also began to guide her career in a new direction.

Chapter 6

MOVING ON

"**E**ven when I was little, I knew I was meant to perform. I would watch specials on TV or videos of Janet [Jackson] or Whitney [Houston], and I would start crying because I was like 'I want that so bad,'" stated Christina.[1]

In December 2000, Christina's *My Reflection*, was broadcast on television and highly praised by the music critics. "The first half-hour of the first Christina Aguilera network special. . .[is] cute as a button. It's sexy. It frontloads all the hits. . . . Essentially it's everything a girl (or boy) could want in an Aguilera special."[2] Over 8 million people watched the program on ABC.

But her life was not entirely upbeat. Christina's abrupt style of dealing with other people had drawn criticism from singers, such as Jessica Simpson. Mariah Carey refused to meet with Christina, although Christina wanted very much to befriend Mariah. And *People* magazine named Christina one of the worst

In December 2000, Christina's talent was broadcast on televisions across America, when ABC aired her musical special, *My Reflection*.

dressed women of the year. She had also developed a nasty reputation at hotels and restaurants for having an arrogant and even rude attitude toward employees.

Nevertheless, Christina's fame and her appearances continued to increase. Early in 2001, she sang a duet with pop star Ricky Martin that became an instant hit.

In 2001, Christina joined other pop stars to record a song titled "Lady Marmalade" for the film *Moulin Rouge*, starring actress Nicole Kidman. "Lady Marmalade" was a remake of a classic song first recorded by signing legend Patti Labelle's girl group, LaBelle, in 1974. This soundtrack

Ricky Martin

Ricky Martin was born in San Juan, Puerto Rico, in 1971. As a child, he appeared in commercials and later joined the singing group Menudo. After leaving the group in 1989, he released his first album *Ricky Martin* in 1988 and a second album, *Me Amaras*, in 1989. Following his success as a singer, he appeared in the television show *Getting By*, and in 1995 in the daytime soap opera, *General Hospital*. A year later, he was a star on Broadway in *Les Miserables*.

Meanwhile, Martin continued to release successful albums. An album in 1997 was followed by another in 1998, featuring the hugely popular single, "The Cup of Life." Martin's next single, "Livin' La Vida Loca," made him an international superstar. Winner of a Grammy Award in 1999 for Best Latin Pop Performance, he released a new album in 2000, titled *Sound Loaded*, followed by an album in 2005 and his autobiography, *Me*, in 2010. Two years later, Martin was back on Broadway in *Evita*, the musical about Argentina's famous and controversial leader in the 1950s, Eva Peron.

recording would feature a quartet of pop music's current powerhouses: Christina, Pink, Mýa, and Lil' Kim. Pink later revealed that she did not like Christina. Part of the problem may have been that Christina, whose voice was stronger than the other women, was the final vocalist to perform on the song. This gave her the most important position in "Lady Marmalade." Christina's was also the first name to appear in the credits for "Lady Marmalade." Whether the trouble with the other ladies was due to jealousy or a clash of personalities, listeners couldn't tell there was any trouble at all. The song was a hit, and it won Christina and her fellow divas a Grammy Award for Best Pop Collaboration with Vocals.

When the music video for "Lady Marmalade" was released, Christina appeared wearing very little clothing and an unusual blonde hairstyle. It was a new look for Christina, and many of her fans were not happy with this sexy style. They liked Christina as a "teeny bopper," and in "Lady Marmalade" she seemed to be moving away from her teen-pop image.[3]

Later in the year, she received two awards for *Mi Reflejo* at the *Billboard* Latin Music Awards. She also became a spokesperson for Coke, beginning an advertising rivalry with Britney Spears, who was advertising Pepsi. "Britney Spears and Christina Aguilera have extended their rivalry to the cola wars," proclaimed one newspaper.[4]

By the middle of 2001, "Lady Marmalade" had become the number one song on the *Billboard* Top 100. In September, Christina and the other stars performed

"Lady Marmalade" at the MTV Video Music Awards. These female stars received MTV awards for "Best Video from a Film," and "Video of the Year."

Public and Private Perception

Meanwhile, Christina's personal life seemed to be a continuous mixture of down notes and up notes. She had broken up with boyfriend Jorge Santos. As it turned out, the dancer was unable to maintain a committed relationship with Christina. After breaking up and getting back together repeatedly, the couple finally ended their romance. At the same time, Christina's image as a

Christina had to learn to share the spotlight with (from left) Pink, Lil Kim, and Mýa on the song "Lady Marmalade" in 2001.

pop star was continuing to change. She released a single, titled "Dirrty" that was sexually explicit and seemed to cement the singer's desire to break away from her teen pop image.

"The whole vision for this record was to be really raw and real," she explained. "Just really baring who I really am." As *New York Times* reporter Kelefa Sanneh added, "The young singers who rose to fame during the teen-pop boom are scrambling to stay relevant." Sanneh added that pop stars Pink and Britney Spears were doing the same thing.[5]

Christina's new image was also on display as she celebrated her twenty-first birthday on December 18, 2001. Much like her appearance in the music video of "Dirrty," Christina arrived at the birthday party on a black motorcycle. Then, with cameras recording her arrival, she went through the doors of a posh Hollywood nightclub to enjoy a birthday bash with her friends.

Chapter 7

A NEW IMAGE

"When you're part of a pop phenomenon," Christina said, "you have so many opinions shoved down your throat. People try to tell you what you should do, how you should act, what you should wear, who you should be with. At the time things started happening for me, it was popular to be the squeaky-clean, cookie-cutter pop singer. But that role didn't speak to me because it's so boring and superficial."[1]

For several years, Christina had been telling RCA Records that she wanted to change her pop-star image. But in her early career, when she was still getting started, stardom meant doing what you were told. She had a great voice and used it to sing what her directors and writers told her to sing. But, after becoming a Grammy Award winner and selling millions of records, Christina believed that she was finally in a position to do what she wanted. And that was not being just another pop star.

Her transition had begun with "Lady Marmalade" in 2001. A year later, she released a new album, titled *Stripped*, a statement that announced to her fans and to the rest of the music world that Christina had decided to take a new direction. This would be the real Christina, not a pop-star image created by RCA. Meanwhile she gave herself a new nickname, "Xtina," along with a tattoo on the back of her neck that spelled out "Xtina" for everyone to see.

Most of the songs on *Stripped* were written by Christina herself. They combined pop with R&B as well as dashes of rock, soul, and Latin music. Many of the songs came from her own life experiences, especially her love affair with Jorge Santos.

Songs From *Stripped*

"Loving Me for Me". . . . .her early love for Jorge who accepted her for being her

"Infatuation". . .the early love wears away and nothing takes its place

"Impossible". . .Christina's efforts to love a difficult man

"The Voice Within". . .realizing that you have to be yourself

"Walk Away". . .finally leaving Jorge to go on with the rest of her life

"Beautiful". . .revealing Christina's feelings about herself

But some of Christina's fans were not happy. "Certain people didn't get it, and that's why they didn't get songs on the record," she explained. Many of the songs were written together with songwriter Linda Perry. She had written songs for Pink, which Christina greatly admired. "...I really, really loved the Linda Perry songs," Christina explained. "They had a really personal, real sense about them."[2]

Christina teamed up with gritty songwriter Linda Perry for many of the songs on *Stripped,* an album that was a change from her earlier work.

As *New York Times* reporter Kelefa Sanneh added, "It's a thrill to hear Ms. Aguilera sounding so indignant. The main problem with her first album was that her tough, virtuosic delivery often didn't match the meek songs she was singing—she didn't really seem like a hopeless romantic. . . ."[3]

Christina sang "Infatuation" at the 2002 Olympics. In the summer of 2003 she went on tour with another pop powerhouse and former *Mickey Mouse Club* castmate Justin Timberlake. On the tour, each sang songs from their own hit albums. Timberlake praised Christina's voice as one of the best he had ever heard. The two stars also recorded an album called *Justin and Christina,* to promote their North American tour. Later that year Christina went on a solo tour to Europe, Japan, and Australia. From the *Stripped* introduction, she celebrated her new direction with the words, "Sorry that I speak my mind/Sorry don't do what I'm told."

Although the album received mixed reviews from critics, it reached the top ranks of the US *Billboard* 200. Four years later, over 12 million albums had been sold across the world.

"Dirrty"

Perhaps the most controversial song from the new album was "Dirrty." It was the lead song on the album, and more than any other it let everyone know that Christina Aguilera was becoming a different type of singer. She performed the song during her two tours in 2003. However, it never reached as high on the

US *Billboard* Top 100 as the entire album did. While some critics called it the best song on the *Stripped* album, others did not like it. The lyrics were simple and straightforward, and they were unflinching in announcing the new—but possibly more authentic—Christina Aguilera.

By far the most controversial aspect of "Dirrty" was the music video that Christina made with the rap star, Redman. As the video opened, Christina arrived in a bikini and chaps, riding a motorcycle into a night-club. The video included a large number of dancers, and various parts of the performances were sexually suggestive. "I like to shock," Christina said. "I think it's inspiring. I love to play and experiment, to be as tame or as outlandish as I happen to feel on any given day."[4]

Redman

Reginald Noble was born in Newark, New Jersey in 1970. Known as Redman, he is a rapper, actor, and record producer. In 1992, his first album appeared, titled *Whut? Thee Album*. This was followed two years later by the album, *Dare is a Darkside*, which included the hit song "Rockafella." His third album, *Muddy Waters*, had two singles that reached the *Billboard* 100. In 1999, Redman released an album with Method Man, which went all the way to number three on the *Billboard* 200 chart. Later albums were also very successful, including those released in 2007, 2009, and 2010.

Christina reunited with her former castmate Justin Timberlake in 2003, with a new look and a mature attitude.

But many critics were not impressed with Christina's experimentation. And a lot of her fans did not like the new direction that Christina had taken with her career.

With "Dirrty," Christina was revealing a sexier, more suggestive side. This new side of the singer shocked many of her fans.

Chapter 8

CHRISTINA AND BRITNEY

Ever since the days of *The All New Mickey Mouse Club,* the media have compared the careers of Christina Aguilera and Britney Spears. The two women were close friends during their Mickey Mouse days, and their mothers also became very friendly while both families lived at the Disney studios in Florida.

As time went on, however, and their careers took off, the media tried to create a rivalry between the two singers. Their singing styles were compared, as well as their clothes and their hairstyles. When Britney appeared as a spokesperson for Pepsi and Christina appeared for Coke, the media drew immediate attention to their roles in the "Cola Wars."

At first, Christina tried to resist participating in this rivalry that the media had created, at least in part, to publish interesting stories for the public. She didn't like the comparisons and believed it was unfair of the media to drive a wedge between the two singers. In 2000, for example, an article appeared comparing the albums each singer had sold in the United States, their number one songs, and the number of Grammy awards each had won. At that time, Christina had won her first Grammy, and Britney had yet to win this award. Her first Grammy came in 2005 for her song, "Toxic."

Christina was appalled by the comparisons and explained that Britney felt unfairly treated. As time went on, of course, Britney won more awards. Unfortunately, the rivalry between the two women also increased.

In 2003, for example, Christina criticized Britney for lip-synching her songs when she made appearances at public events. She was only one among many singers who used this technique. But Christina, who always sang live and relied on her strong voice, did not resort to lip-synching. And she did not believe that any other singer should try to fool the public in this way.

"I'm trying to bring back the art in artist," she said. "It's sad because, with technology, art has become so easy to

Music Awards for Britney Spears	
American Music Awards	1
Billboard Music Awards	7
MTV Video Music Awards	6
Teen Choice Awards	8
People's Choice Awards	1
World Music Awards	3
MTV Europe Music Awards	8

In the early days of their solo pop careers, Britney and Christina had to contend with unfair comparisons from critics and fans alike.

Music Awards for Christina Aguilera	
ALMA Awards (Best Latin Vocalist)	2
Billboard Music Awards	1
Grammy Awards	5
Latin Grammy Awards	1
People's Choice Awards	1
Teen Choice Awards	2

manufacture—you don't even have to sing anymore." She was referring to an awards ceremony where the singers, including Britney, were not singing live. "Who knows what happened exactly? She was *supposed* to sing live. These people aren't artists, they're just performers. . . ."[1]

Meanwhile, Christina's image had become even more controversial. In November 2003, she appeared at the Europe Music Awards Show. Christina was dressed as a Catholic nun and sang "Beautiful" with the National Youth Choir of Scotland. Some believed Christina was being disrespectful to religion: It almost seemed as if she was making fun of a nun's vocation. She also managed to win several prestigious awards that year, including Best Video Award for "Dirrty," and Sexiest Woman of the Year from *Maxim* magazine. Her award from *Maxim* really didn't fit with the nun's image she tried to portray at the Europe Music Awards Show.

Britney, on the other hand, had tried to retain more of the pop-star image that she had created as a younger singer—one far less controversial than Christina's. As time went on, however, Britney's image also changed.

Marriage

The conflict between Christina and Britney grew deeper in 2004, when Christina was asked to replace Britney as the spokesperson for Skechers footwear. When Britney was dropped because of a lawsuit involving the singer and the company, Christina was selected to replace her. She brought her own somewhat racier style to the brand as its new spokeswoman.

In January 2004, Britney had married longtime friend Jason Alexander in Las Vegas, Nevada. Spears had made the decision on the spur of the moment, and at 3:30 in the morning of January 3, the couple was

The Kiss

In 2003, Christina appeared with Britney Spears and Madonna at the MTV Video Music Awards. As Christina and Britney sang a duet of Madonna's 1984 smash controversial hit "Like a Virgin," who should show up but the original artist herself!

Emerging from an enormous wedding cake on stage, Madonna made her grand appearance. Then, seemingly unrehearsed, Britney walked right up to Madonna and gave her a long kiss on the lips. Shortly afterward, Christina, dressed in a wedding gown in homage to the original video and with her hair dyed black, went up to Madonna and placed a kiss on her lips. The scene was completely unexpected by the audience and may have shocked some of Christina's fans. But it symbolized a new direction for the star and for her performances.

driven in a green stretch limousine to A Little White Wedding Chapel. This was a famous Las Vegas location for couples to marry. However, Britney and Jason were not permitted to get married until they went to the county courthouse to obtain a marriage license. After paying for the license, they returned to the wedding chapel to be married in a short ceremony. Britney was wearing a baseball hat and jeans.

According to Charlotte Richards, who owned the wedding chapel, "They weren't dressed in wedding attire, but it was very romantic and there was a feeling of love between them. They appeared to be extremely happy. . . . I thought it was a marriage that would last forever."[2] But the marriage lasted only 55 hours. Both the bride and groom decided they didn't want to be married. Instead, they hired a lawyer to help arrange an annulment. And by January 5, the marriage was over.

Christina was highly critical of the entire affair. What's more, she had decided to do things quite differently for her own marriage. Christina had met Jordan Bratman in 2002. He was an executive in the music business and a consultant for Universal Pictures. At a hotel in Big Sur, on the coast of California, Jordan had proposed to Christina on February 11, 2005.

Meanwhile, the relationship with Jordan had been accompanied by a new look for the singer. Christina took on the appearance of blonde-haired film legend Marilyn Monroe. She recorded a new song, "A Song for You," with jazz pianist Herbie Hancock, who praised her

Christina married music marketing executive Jordan Bratman on November 19, 2005. Christina has said the marriage grounded her.

singing and her professionalism. Before the wedding, Bratman and Christina gave each other a new tattoo. Hers read "I am my beloved's and my beloved is mine."

Unlike Britney, Christina wore a traditional wedding gown for the ceremony that took place in Napa Valley, California in November of 2005. And her diamond, Christina said, was large and especially designed for her—unlike Britney's. After the ceremony, her band played traditional songs, like songwriter Duke Ellington's "In a Sentimental Mood," and "At Last," which had been sung by vocalist Etta James. Christina especially meant this song for her husband. "At last," Christina seemed to have found the man whom she had looked for during much of her life.

Chapter 9

GIVING BACK

The latest statistics on domestic violence in the United States paint a grim picture:

- The number one cause of injury to women is domestic violence.

- Domestic violence claims another female victim every nine seconds.

- As many as 10 million children see some form of domestic violence annually.

- Reducing domestic violence is the highest priority among most women.[1]

Perhaps no one is more aware of the problems associated with domestic violence than Christina Aguilera. She grew up in a home where her father regularly abused her mother. And she witnessed many of these incidents herself.

For years, Christina had supported a center for domestic abuse in Pittsburgh, one of the many places where she grew up. Then, in 2006, she announced plans to start a new shelter for victims of domestic abuse. These are women who decide to flee their homes instead of submitting themselves and their children to continued violence. Though safe from the original harm, they face a difficult transition to a new life.

"Some of these women leave their homes without anything," Christina said. "They just grab the kids and get out of the situation. And so a lot of these women have nothing, and they have to start from scratch."[2]

In 2007, Christina joined with film actress Nicole Kidman in a campaign to "End Violence Against Women." At the start of each of Christina's concerts, fans were asked to watch a public service advertisement about domestic violence. This was part of a worldwide campaign to bring an end to domestic abuse.

As another element of her campaign, Aguilera spoke out about US Army installations, which she called a "hotbed of domestic abuse."[3] As the singer put it, "We lived on Army bases when I was little, and it (domestic violence) was happening a lot. I was surrounded with domestic violence, not only in my home but my friends."[4] Christina has written about the problem of domestic abuse in several of her songs, including "Oh Mother." As she put it: "It's therapeutic for me to talk about it. It gives me a reason to understand why I went through what I did."[5]

World Charity Work

Christina's charity work runs the gamut from helping AIDS (Autoimmune Deficiency Syndrome) victims to those suffering from hunger. Along with other celebrities

Christina was a celebrity spokesmodel for MAC cosmetic's Viva Glam campaign, which benefits the MAC AIDS fund.

such as Boy George and rap star Missy Elliot, she joined a campaign sponsored by MAC cosmetics in 2004 to fight AIDS. Her message was that young people should take no risks. That year, five million people had contracted AIDS, and almost half of them were under twenty-five years old—like most of Christina's fans.

In 2010, Christina became an ambassador for the United Nations (UN) World Food Program (WFP). As part of her work, she traveled to nations around the globe, visiting with struggling families and spearheading the campaign against world hunger. Every six seconds, a child dies of hunger. "For just 25 cents a day, we can feed a child in school and be part of the solution," Aguilera explained. "In my travels for the World Food Program, I've seen first-hand how that meal changes the life of a child. . . ."[6] In 2012, Christina was given a Leadership Award by the WFP for her work publicizing its message.

In an interview with *Redbook* magazine, Christina talked about some of the women and children she visited in Africa and South America. "I just wanted to hug this young woman Concepcion whom I met in a Guatemalan village. She's 25 years old and has a little daughter and a second baby on the way. She has no job, no money, and her husband just left her. The only food she receives is from WFP."[7]

Christina continued: "I met this little girl in a school at the epicenter of the Haiti earthquake. . . .I was so impressed by how eager all the children were to learn.

In 2011, Christina appeared in a public service announcement for Yum! Brands' World Hunger Relief campaign to stop world hunger.

Without their school lunches, they wouldn't be able to concentrate on their studies."[8]

In 2014 alone Christina helped raise $37 million in her campaigns to help needy people around the world. It exemplified what one person could accomplish, especially if that person was a star with worldwide name recognition. Like some other great entertainers, Christina had not forgotten where she started—even with all the success that she had subsequently achieved. This enabled her to empathize with those in need across the globe.

Chapter 10

BACK TO BASICS

In 2006, Christina released a new album called *Back to Basics*. The music recalled some of the great jazz hits from the 1930s to the 1990s. These were played by performers such as trumpeter Louis Armstrong and bandleader Duke Ellington, and sung by vocalists like Billie Holiday, Etta James, Aretha Franklin, and Ella Fitzgerald.

Inspired by these hits, Christina wrote the album's songs herself. The songs also described her experiences growing up; her first love, Jorge; and her marriage to Jordan Bratman. Some of them were produced by her friend Linda Perry, whose song "Beautiful" had been a tremendous hit for Christina. Perry had encouraged the singer to put more emotion into her performances instead of relying so much on her powerful voice and loud electronic effects.

Christina's new album featured the song, "Ain't No Other Man," produced by Perry. On the bluesy/jazzy tune, Christina sang with deep emotion about her love for her husband Jordan Bratman.

On her "Back to Basics" tour in 2006, Christina was inspired by great American jazz standards from the twentieth century.

Another song, the devastating "Hurt," described her feelings after losing someone whom she deeply loved. The lyrics for "The Right Man" were written about Christina's relationship with her father, Fausto. Other songs included "Slow Down Baby," "Here to Stay," "Back in the Day," and "On Our Way." Christina actually had enough songs to release a double album. But RCA was opposed to the idea because double albums cost twice as much to produce, and in addition they often did poorly in term of sales. But Christina insisted, and the record company finally agreed to her demands.

She was right! The album immediately went to the top of the music charts in the United States and in many other countries. The experience taught Christina to trust her instincts—and her talent.

Christina is a "fighter," one reporter wrote, and "she's fighting for the right to be what she already is: a pop star. She's demanding that she be allowed to do her job. This demand is the main theme of *Back to Basics. . . .*" She had watched other pop stars decline in popularity and lose their vocal ranges. "To Ms. Aguilera, this state of affairs means one thing: market share up for grabs. She seems intent on establishing herself as a modern anomaly, a pop singer who really—really, really—sings."[1]

In 2006, Christina also had the chance to spend time with one of her heroes, singer Etta James. They appeared in photographs for the fashion magazine *In Style*, and talked about their mutual admiration for each other. Etta praised Christina for her wonderful voice and also

Linda Perry

Born in Springfield, Massachusetts, in 1965, Linda Perry eventually moved to San Francisco, where her big voice became the trademark of her performances. At the beginning, Perry was performing on the San Francisco streets before composing "Down on Your Face," and joining the band, 4 Non Blondes, in 1989. Her voice and her songs were featured on the band's first album, *Bigger, Better, Faster, More!*, released in 1992. Perry resigned from the band two years later to pursue a solo career.

Perry produced her first solo album, *In Flight*, in 1996. Her second album, *After Hours*, followed three years later. Meanwhile, she continued to write songs that were performed by other artists, including Christina Aguilera on her album *Stripped*. In 2006, Perry accompanied Aguilera on the piano for her performance of "Hurt" at the MTV Video Music Awards. She also worked as songwriter and producer of *Missundaztood*, by the rock singer Pink, while working with a variety of other singers, including Celine Dion, Alicia Keys, Enrique Iglesias, and Courtney Love. In 2011, Perry released the album, *8 Songs About a Girl*, featuring her band, Deep Dark Robot.

Perry married actress and talk show host Sara Gilbert in 2014, and their son Rhodes was born the following year.

In 2012, Christina had the great honor of singing at the funeral of one of her heroes, blues legend Etta James.

for her feisty personality, much like Etta's own. Etta also compared Christina to vocalist Billie Holiday, the great blues singer. "I've never seen a girl as tough as you sing, as little as you are. . . ," Etta said.[2]

Chapter 11

THE NEXT STAGE

In 2007, Christina won a Grammy Award for "Ain't No Other Man." She had also achieved a level of success reached by few other singers—multiple platinum recordings. "Multiple platinum" is a music industry measure that signifies one million sales for a single or an album. Yet, in becoming phenomenally successful, Christina had also gained a reputation as an aggressive, pushy woman, who might stop at nothing to get what she wanted.

But this perception did not deter her. The same year, she released a music video of "Candyman" from the *Back to Basics* album. This video showed three versions of Christina—as a brunette, a blonde, and a redhead—dancing to music from the 1940s.

In 2007, she also headlined her own tour, featuring singles from *Back to Basics*. The *New York Times* reporter Kelefa Sanneh wrote: "The implicit message of 'Back to Basics,' the album and the tour, is that Ms. Aguilera has moved beyond the teen-pop fluff that made her a star. She listens to serious music now. . .because she's a serious singer. . . .But none of this explains why paying fans should have to spend precious minutes watching a video of Ms. Aguilera writhing in her undergarments. . . ."[1]

The new album was not as successful as some of her earlier efforts. The same reporter commented, after attending the concert: ". . .it was clear that the blockbuster hits from 'Stripped' still work. The crowd sang along. . . .And if you really want to stop a show properly few songs will get the job done better than 'Beautiful. . . .'"[2]

To ring in the new year, Christina performed the single "Candyman" on *Dick Clark's New Year's Rockin' Eve* in 2007.

Meanwhile, the singer recorded a song for *Instant Karma: The Amnesty International Campaign to Save Darfur*. Amnesty International is an organization devoted to exposing civil rights abuses around the world in areas such as Darfur—a region located in the Sudan, Africa. At the same time, Christina was endorsing a new perfume, releasing "Slow Down Baby" as a single from her *Back to Basics* album, and appearing on the Emmy Awards show to honor outstanding television programs and stars.

All that time, Christina was pregnant with her first child. No one knew outside her family until celebrity Paris Hilton announced the good news at a party in Las Vegas. "Congratulations to the most beautiful pregnant woman in the world," she said. "You're gorgeous."[3] By this time, Christina was five months pregnant. In November, a picture of Christina appeared on the cover of *Marie Claire* magazine, pregnant and showing her burgeoning stomach unclothed.

Nevertheless, the pregnancy had not prevented Christina from continuing a whirlwind career. She had flown to New Zealand and Australia, although the tour had worn her out.

When she appeared in Pittsburgh to perform songs from her *Back to Basics* album, one reporter wrote: "Aguilera, widely known as the young pop diva who can actually sing, placed herself in the heart of a major arena spectacle with 20 people on stage. . . .The suspense built into the evening was how she would appear on stage next and what she would be wearing. She came by moving staircase, carousel horse, couch rising from the floor and, most dramatically, on one of those circus wheels that doubles as a target for the knife thrower. . . .the voice? What else—big and full of gutsy bravado. . . .As a performer she lights up a stage with a mess of blond hair, bright red lipstick and sexy dance moves."[4]

A New Family Life

Finally on January 12, 2008, Christina gave birth to a son, Max Liron Bratman. He was a small baby, just over 6 pounds. On her website, Christina announced Max's birth, writing: "Today is a very joyful and special day for Jordan and I as we welcome our first son into this world."[5] Only a short time later, Christina was appearing on the daytime talk show *The Ellen DeGeneres Show* telling the audience about nursing her baby. She described giving birth as the best experience of her life.

Christina Rolls Her Eyes

Graphic Interchange Format (GIF) has become a new method of communication on computers and iPhones. This consists of animated graphics that contain a message. According to the *New York Times*, one user "who wanted a friend to stop sending her pictures of food responded with a GIF—an animated image. . .of Christina Aguilera rolling her eyes, waving her hand and soundlessly mouthing 'PLEASE STOP.'"[6] She must have thought that Christina's reputation for being catty would capture her feelings perfectly.

Christina swaddled her newborn son, Max, in the American flag for a 2008 public service announcement for Rock the Vote.

In order to spend more time with Max, Christina had set up a recording studio in the large home that she and her husband had purchased in Hollywood. Christina did not want any time to go by before creating more hits. She wanted to capitalize on the success of the *Back to Basics* video *"Live and Down Under,"* presenting her tour in New Zealand and Australia, which was the top DVD in the United States after its release in early 2008. During the summer, Christina appeared with her son, singing "America the Beautiful" in a public service announcement designed to persuade people to go out and vote. However, she was criticized by some people for using Max to get publicity and at the same time violating the accepted standards of good motherhood. But that didn't bother Christina.

It also didn't stop her from composing a new hit song released in 2008, "Keeps Gettin' Better." The aggressive, exciting song was written by Christina and Linda Perry.

Unlike the album *Back to Basics,* the music had a futuristic sound. Christina did not simply want to repeat what she had done before; instead she wanted to move forward in a new direction. Later at the MTV Video Music Awards in September, she performed the new song in a leather costume while wearing a mask. It was a futuristic new look for Christina to go with her futuristic new song.

A month later, Christina was on the road again; this time, performing in London.

Chapter 12

SLIDING DOWNHILL

In April 2010, Christina released a single titled, "Not Myself Tonight." Instead of featuring her strong voice, the song featured electronica—that is, electronic enhancements of the music that gave it almost a digital sound. The new song was not very successful. As one of her friends put it, "Christina gave up her famous belting because she said she was bored of it, and that was the downfall of her career."[1]

Indeed, the music was not her usual fare—either in sound or the lyrics that usually sprang from her own heartfelt experiences. Instead she had begun to look and sound like other pop stars, such as the increasingly popular Lady Gaga.

In June, Christina released the album *Bionic,* which included the single "Not Myself Tonight," as well as the title song, "Bionic."

Christina's new album debuted as number one on the charts, and then almost immediately started dropping in sales. ". . .it [the drop in sales] suggested fans had initially purchased the album with high hopes because it had her name attached to it, but that the word had spread quickly that it didn't live up to their lofty expectations," said one writer.[2] Photographs of Christina on the album seemed like an attempt to make her resemble Lady Gaga, and *Bionic* contained sexual content that went far beyond Christina's earlier albums.

Personal Disappointments

Not only did Christina's music career seem to be going downhill, her personal life had also gone off the tracks. In 2010, she and her husband Jordan Bratman decided

Christina's Homes

In 2007, Christina Aguilera bought a huge home in Beverly Hills, California, that was worth several million dollars. To give her more time with her son Max, Christina built a recording studio in the mansion so she could record at home. After Aguilera's divorce from Jordan Bratman, the couple put the house up for sale at a price of $13.5 million in 2011. The house remained on the market for approximately two years before Christina finally sold it. Then she bought a $10 million mansion in 2013. The huge home measured 11,000 square feet, (1,022 meters) and included marble floors and a large swimming pool. Her nearest neighbors in Beverly Hills are socialite and DJ Paris Hilton and actor Charlie Sheen. For Christina, whose fortune is listed between $100 million and $130 million, the price of her new home will barely affect her financial net worth.

For 2010's *Bionic,* Christina tried a new style—both musically and sartorially. Unfortunately, fans and critics didn't respond.

to divorce, after five years of marriage. "Things were so unhealthy and unhappy for both Jordan and me, I knew I had to end it. I really didn't want to hurt Jordan, and I felt torn about splitting. When you're unhappy in your marriage, your children are the ones who suffer. That's the last thing I wanted for my son."[3] Christina would later reflect, "[2010] was a rough year. Between my divorce and the other things I went through, a lot happened. It's hard for anyone to go through that in public. But when you're a celebrity and under a microscope, it's 58 million times harder. I grew an even thicker skin after that hard year."[4]

Near the end of the year, Christina tried her hand at film acting. Although she had experience on television as a young child, and she had performed in countless music videos, for the first time she took a starring role in a Hollywood movie. In Burlesque, Christina played Ali, a young woman who leaves her home in the hopes of succeeding in a career as a singer in Los Angeles. Eventually, Ali gets a job as a waitress at the Burlesque Lounge. The Lounge is owned by a woman named Tess, played by Cher. Ali finally convinces Tess to let her audition as a singer on stage and becomes a hit with the audiences.

Director Steve Antin said that he believed the part of Ali was perfect for Christina. "I had this instinct about her. I had seen her on Saturday Night Live doing something very difficult. I don't think people realize how tough it is to be funny in a live element like that. I

Cher

Cherilyn Sarkisian, later known as Cher, was born in California in 1946. At the age of eighteen, she married twenty-nine-year-old Salvatore "Sonny" Bono and the two sang together as the duo Sonny and Cher throughout the 1960s. They also starred in their own hugely popular television variety show, *The Sonny and Cher Show*, during the early 1970s. The couple divorced in 1975.

Sonny later became a US congressman, and Cher became known for her unusual costumes and hit songs. Cher is also a gifted actress, appearing on Broadway in 1982 and in several films afterward. These included *Silkwood* in 1983, *Mask* in 1985, and *Moonstruck* in 1987. For *Moonstruck*, Cher won an Oscar Award for Best Actress. She continued releasing new songs in the 2000s and launched a long musical tour, which she called "Living Proof: The Farewell Tour." From 2008 to 2011, Cher headlined her own show in Las Vegas at Caesars Palace. And in 2013, Cher released her new album, *Closer to the Truth*, followed by a tour in 2014.

During the filming of *Burlesque*, Cher and Christina reportedly developed a strong friendship. Talking about Cher, Christina said, "She's just such an unbelievable presence and person and been there, done everything before any of us came along. You know, I admire that. I truly respect that."[5]

Christina costarred with entertainment legend Cher in 2010's *Burlesque.* Aguilera got the chance to act and sing in the film.

knew she could do this based on her instincts in those seemingly simple, but really incredibly difficult comedy skits. I knew she could do any of the comedy in the movie and all of the drama."[6]

Unfortunately, many critics did not like the film. As one critic put it, "Oh *Burlesque*...where to start? The latest entry in the musical genre doesn't break any new ground, hits every movie cliché note, and makes singing

※ 79 ※

its praises impossible. If you're a big Christina Aguilera fan, then *Burlesque* is satisfying enough. But Aguilera's singing is the only thing worthwhile in this campy, sanitized peek backstage at a burlesque lounge."[7]

By all accounts, *Burlesque* was a flop, even with Christina's singing to bolster it. Even though the movie has since become a camp classic, Christina has never returned to the big screen in a starring role.

Chapter 13

In 2011, *The Voice* debuted on the television network NBC. A reality talent show, *The Voice* features celebrity singers who serve as coaches for a group of talented young unknown artists hoping to break through. Each celebrity acts as a mentor to a team of singers, who compete throughout the season through weekly eliminations. At the end of the season, one singer is selected by the television audience as the winner. The winner of *The Voice* receives $100,000 and a record contract with Universal Music Group.

Although it was certainly not the first televised talent show, *The Voice* differed from its competitors, such as *American Idol,* in several ways. First, unlike *Idol,* contestants did not have to fall within a certain (namely young) age range. Second, contestants were first selected during "blind auditions" in which judges could not see

Christina's talent has taken her from a contestant on *Star Search* to a judge on NBC's vocal competition *The Voice.*

them. This meant that the contestants' voices, not their images or looks, would drive the competition.

Christina began appearing as a celebrity coach in 2011 when *The Voice* debuted. The other coaches were rock band Maroon 5 lead singer Adam Levine, relatively unknown country singer Blake Shelton, and offbeat singer and producer CeeLo Green. The host of the show was Carson Daly. Aguilera remained on the show for the first three seasons. Then she took a leave of absence, returning in Season Five and in Season Eight—2014.

In January and February, young artists audition at various locations across the United States. These include Chicago, New York, Miami, Nashville, Los Angeles, and Seattle. They then perform for the coaches in Los Angeles. The coaches are seated in chairs facing away from the stage. If a coach is impressed with the artist's performance, he or she presses a button to indicate interest in the performer. Pressing the button turns the coach's chair around so that he or she is facing the stage. If more than one coach turns around, the contestant gets to choose which coach he or she wants to work with. From the auditions, each coach then puts together a team of performers. The coaches then mentor their performers and prepare them to win a series of competitions during an entire season.

In the last phase, performers compete in the finals, and one of them is selected by an audience of viewers— voting via online or by telephone, text message, an app, or iTunes. Coaches are also competing for as many

Christina's Clothing

In 2011, Christina Aguilera announced that she was planning to introduce her own line of clothing. The new line was a joint venture in cooperation with the large Brazilian department store, C&A. Many celebrities put their names on clothing lines without being involved in the clothes themselves. At an appearance in São Paolo, Brazil, however, Christina promised that she would play a large role in the design and manufacture of her line.

But as Christina has pointed out in the past, clothing is only part of her distinctive look. As she has adapted different styles over the years, she has changed her hair color, makeup—even the era she is emulating. She even relies on unique perfumes to enhance her appearance. However, Christina also tries to take good care of her skin and hair. No matter how tired she may be, she makes sure to remove her makeup before she goes to bed. And she always—always!—moisturizes her skin and conditions her hair.

members of their team as possible to finish first, second, or third.

Although not one of Christina's team members ever won the contest—Jacquie Lee, who was on her team—finished as the runner-up during Season Five, 2013.

One reporter said that Christina's appearance on *The Voice* was a key factor in making it a hit. "Years from now, Christina Aguilera will be remembered for her glamour, her scandalous take on femme-pop and her. . .voice. But she should also be remembered as the person who almost single-handedly reshaped music competition reality programming."

The reporter went on to point out that although her last album *Bionic* and her film *Burlesque* had not been very successful, "Ms. Aguilera was an undeniable contemporary pop star, and her presence elevated those [that is, the other coaches] around her." They were not as well-known.[1]

From the beginning, *The Voice* was phenomenally successful, attracting a large number of adults in the 18 to 49 age range. By its second season, approximately 18 million viewers were watching the show. "To be given the opportunity to help shape new artists' careers and mentor them to see their dreams come to fruition is a task I welcome with open arms," Christina said.[2]

The Voice: Season Eight Finale

On May 19, 2015, the live finale of *The Voice* aired on NBC. The show began,

> A new star will be placed in the musical sky tonight, a bright new light to shine and sing and fill our hearts for what we hope will be a long, long time. Tonight we crown *The Voice* Season Eight champion. The stage is set, the seats are filled, the coaches are dressed in their finest, and our four finalists are bubbling with excitement. . . .[3]

The coaches that season were Christina, Adam Levine, Blake Shelton, and superstar producer Pharrell Williams. The four finalists were: Koryn Hawthorne, Joshua Davis, Meghan Linsey, and Sawyer Fredericks.

The Voice's Winning Contestants

Winners of *The Voice* have been:

Javier Colon
Jermaine Paul
Cassadee Pope
Danielle Bradbery
Tessanne Chin
Josh Kaufman
Craig Wayne Boyd
Sawyer Fredericks

Coach Adam Levine was up first to talk about his finalist Joshua Davis. Davis asked other artists who had been competitors, but who not made the finals, to come on stage to join him in the song, "She Talks to Angels." Later Levine sang with his group Maroon 5, a single titled "This Summer's Gonna Hurt."

After Davis, singer Meghan Trainor appeared on stage. She sang her own song, "Dear Future Husband," accompanying herself on the ukulele. Sawyer Fredericks, the next finalist, appeared with John Fogerty, head of the popular band, Credence Clearwater Revival. Fogerty sang one of the band's great hits, "Born on the Bayou." He was joined part way through the song by Fredericks, and they sang "Bad Moon Rising," and "Have You Ever Seen the Rain?," two hits from the past.

Finalist Joshua Davis came forward to duet with star Sheryl Crow, singing her hit "Give It to Me." Later in the show, the four coaches teamed up to sing a hit from the late R&B singing great, B.B. King, "The Thrill is Gone."

Near the end of the show, host Carson Daly finally introduced the order of the four finalists. The countdown began with Koryn Hawthorne, who finished fourth, Joshua Davis, who finished third, Meghan Linsey, second, and finally, Sawyer Fredericks, the winner of *The Voice* contest.

Personal Ups and Downs

Aguilera's appearance on *The Voice* was not only good for the show, but also for her own career. And, by this time, Christina's career needed a boost. 2010 had been the first time she had experienced failure—with her

Christina's Hair on *The Voice*

When Christina Aguilera appeared on *The Voice* for its third season, she wanted to make sure that her hair would be noticed and remembered by fans of the show. As a result, she asked hairstylist Mark Townsend to introduce strawberry highlights to her hair, which at the time already had distinguishing red tips. With a curling iron, he also wrapped part of her hair in a bun to one side of her head. "To add some fun to her hair," Townsend added, "I braided the whole right side of her hair into several twists so the pink color would show in the front."[4] The style was wholly unique and memorable, indeed, even for this style chameleon!

Christina's Makeup

One of the most distinctive elements of the Christina Aguilera look is her bright red lipstick. This is not a single color, but a mix of different shades that Christina blends together, almost like a fine painter. She layers together a cranberry red shade with a blue-red shade to achieve the final result. Each shade is applied in several layers. The result is a lipstick that withstands water, kissing, rubbing, and smearing. This enables Christina to enhance her appearance when she sings and dances on stage, stars in a film like *Burlesque*, or coaches the talented singers that compete on *The Voice*.

album *Bionic* and her first feature film, *Burlesque*. Still, she was not only able to admit her failures, but also she knew how to learn from them:

> I was sad, but I'm still glad that I did the movie. During production, I was going through a lot of self-discovery. As a quote-unquote-pop star, you have your entourage with you at all times. When you enter and leave a place, backstage, even at home—you always have your team. On the movie set, I didn't have anyone around me. . . . After the movie, I grew out of being that little girl: I became an adult.[5]

Early in 2011, before joining *The Voice,* she had appeared at the Super Bowl to sing the National Anthem. The appearance turned into a disaster, however, when she sang some of the words incorrectly. Instead of singing "O'er the ramparts we watched were so gallantly

Christina returned to the Super Bowl in 2011. This time, she sang the notoriously difficult *Star-Spangled Banner,* not without incident.

streaming," Christina sang "What so proudly we watched at the twilight's last reaming." It was a major embarrassment for her.

As she later explained, "Everything on the field at the Super bowl was vividly bright, and I was having a moment. I got lost in the emotion of being there and I messed up the lyrics to the song."[6] She added: "I can only hope that everyone could feel my love for this country and that the true spirit of the anthem still came through."[7]

After the event, Christina went to dinner with a new boyfriend, Matthew Rutler. He had worked on

Christina's troubles continued when she tripped onstage at the Grammys. Rumors swirled that the singer had an alcohol problem.

the production of her film, *Burlesque.* ". . .Matt and I laughed about how I'd made myself into a Trivial Pursuit question: 'In 2011 what female singer flubbed the lyrics to the national anthem?'"[8]

But Christina's problems weren't over. At the Grammy Awards ceremony in February, she tripped and almost fell on stage. Then the following month, she and Matt Rutler were stopped in their car by the police and charged with driving while under the influence of alcohol. They were arrested and shortly afterward released.

For Christina, the time had come to look ahead, not backward.

Chapter 14

LOTUS

"**B**y pursuing my first passion of music during the break, I am also able to come back and offer even more to my team on *The Voice* in the future."[1] This was Christina's announcement in 2011 as she left the television show to devout herself to her own music. After all, this was her first passion.

The following year on November 9, 2012, she released her new album, *Lotus.* Before the entire album was released, several singles from the album had already appeared with positive results.

Christina had returned to songs that came from her own heart and her own experience. The style of singing as well as the lyrics and the songs marked a tremendous change from *Bionic.* And the title song signaled that Christina was returning from failure to begin a new phase of her career. She was like an emerging lotus flower.

Songs from the album included "Empty Words," "Best of Me," and the ballad, "Blank Page," in which she looked back on her failed marriage. From her experience as a judge and mentor on *The Voice*, Christina composed "Sing For Me" about her efforts to guide and enhance the careers of young singers. And with Blake Shelton, a country singer and one of the other celebrity mentors on the show, Christina sang "Just a Fool."

While the album was well received by her fans, it was not the blockbuster that other albums had been. One critic wrote, "Christina Aguilera is easily one of contemporary music's best voices. She's got pipes that music lovers need to hear at a time when. . .radio features studio-enhanced vocals and award shows are full of lip-synching. That's why her fifth album, *Lotus*, is somewhat disappointing—not because it isn't good, but because it isn't great." The reviewer went on to say that *Lotus* was far better than *Bionic* "but not as satisfying as her first three releases."[2]

Nevertheless, the album was a success.

A Song With Pitbull

In 2013, Christina joined rap superstar Pitbull, whose real name is Armando Christian Perez, for a duet called "Feel this Moment." The high-energy dance number urged listeners to take a break and, well, feel the moment.

Christina paired up with Cuban-American rapper Pitbull in 2013 for the catchy anthem "Feel This Moment," a song they performed at the Billboard Music Awards.

Xtina the Mom

Christina Aguilera may not always be known for her humility. But when it comes to raising a new baby, she recognized her shortcomings as well as her strengths. "It's hard to know you won't have all the right answers at the right times," she admitted. "And 'mom guilt' is the worst thing ever. But you have to surrender and let go, knowing you're doing your very best and no one loves them, or wants what's best for them more than you."[5]

New Sources of Joy

Not only had Christina righted the ship of her music career, her personal life had also taken a decided turn for the better. She and fiancé Matt Rutler welcomed their new baby girl, Summer Rain, into the world in 2014. "We had an immediate calm bond," the singer said, "and I fell unexpectedly connected to her and her spirit."[3]

Christina added that being a parent and a full-time entertainer was not easy. "It's definitely not easy juggling work and motherhood," she explained, "as being a parent is a full-time job within itself. You just have to make it work for you. My life has so many different moving parts, but my kids are the center focal piece, and everything else shifts around them."[4]

After a painful divorce, Christina found love once again. In 2014, she became engaged to Matthew Rutler.

Chapter 15

THE FUTURE OF A SINGING SENSATION

Christina returned to lead a team on *The Voice* for the 2015 season. In honor of the season's last episode, or season finale, producers aired a video that showed Christina like we'd never seen her. To the delight of the audience and her fellow judges, Christina performed hilarious impressions of some of America's most famous singers, including Miley Cyrus, Lady Gaga, and Britney Spears. *Hollywood Life* raved, "Christina Aguilera is a master celebrity impersonator!.... Her impressions are guaranteed to make you LOL!.... Christina Aguilera is one funny lady!"[1]

This was Christina's first season back on the show, following a leave of absence of two years. In March of that year, she appeared in several episodes of the ABC program *Nashville*. Christina wore her hair black for the part of Jade. While working on the set, she tweeted friends, "Jade's been busy studying her lines. . . .Look at all that hair," she added, posting a picture of herself. "Having lots of fun on the set of #Nashville. More to come!"[2]

In April, Christina appeared at the Academy of Country Music Awards in Dallas, Texas. She appeared

Scentsational Christina

Beginning in 2004, Christina launched a series of perfumes under her own name. These included *Xpose* in Europe, followed by *Christina Aguilera* in 2007. This perfume became the top seller in Great Britain and Germany. Christina described it as having a fruity smell. Her other fragrances include:

Inspire	2008
Christina Aguilera by Night	2009
Royal Desire	2010
Red Sin	2012

Her fragrances have also won numerous awards across Europe. "I am very passionate about all the perfumes that I have created and am thrilled that my fans and industry leaders enjoy them as much as I do," Christina said.[3]

Looking back on her own childhood, Christina recalled that she was always interested in perfumes and fragrances. "Growing up, I used to play with all the fragrances in my mother's vanity. She had a taste for musky, sensual scents."[4]

Christina's line of fragrances have been incredibly successful. "Inspire" is her third fragrance but the first to be released in the United States.

with the country-pop group Rascal Flatts and sang "Shotgun" from the *Nashville* show. She also was awarded a Grammy for her collaboration with the group A Great Big World for the heartfelt song "Say Something." These were only two of her stops for 2015. Christina's tour dates for the year included, the United States, Europe, Canada, and Australia.

Earlier that year, Christina had opened the National Basketball Association (NBA) All-Star game at Madison Square Garden in New York. She sang traditional songs to celebrate the Big Apple, like "On Broadway," and "New York State of Mind," and then performed with the famous dance group, the Rockettes, singing "Empire State of Mind." One critic called the performance "masterful."[5]

It seemed that Christina was back!

Chapter 16

THE ELEMENTS OF SUCCESS

What has enabled Christina Aguilera to become such a success? And is there anything we can learn from her experiences that might be instructive for us?

Christina's path to stardom probably started with an innate singing ability that she inherited from her mother. Shelly was a musician who played both the piano and violin. Her mother, Delcie, had even encouraged Shelly to play in the Youth Symphony Orchestra. Shelly enjoyed music and passed on this passion to her daughter. Frequently the daughters and sons of talented parents inherit some of this talent themselves.

Ironically, this talent was honed and shaped in a very unstable household. It is not always the security of a happy family that provides the best atmosphere for a child's later success. In Christina's case, the conflicts between her parents forced her to find an escape that would help her cope with this situation. For Christina, that escape was music.

As a very small girl, she began listening to singers that she liked and singing the songs that they sung—Julie Andrews, Billie Holiday, and Etta James inspired her. But it was also Christina's single-mindedness in pursuing her dream of becoming a singer that helped her succeed.

Although Christina's family endured some tough times, she has always had the support of her sister, Rachel, and mother, Shelly.

This dream began when she was still a child; it helped her through the difficult years of living with parents who fought regularly, and it sustained her as she grew older.

Christina had absolutely convinced herself that she could succeed. As she once explained, Shelly was not the conventional stage mother who pushed her daughter to perform. It was Christina who kept asking her Mom to find places where she could sing. It might be in the neighborhood, at local music stores, or at parties. Overnight, it seemed, she became known as "the little girl with the big voice." When other girls her age came over and asked her to come outside and play, Christina often refused. She preferred instead to concentrate on her singing and on her music.

This type of single-mindedness, almost an obsession, lies behind the success of many great stars. Early on, they form a vision of what they can become—often born from unpleasant surroundings. The vision offers them an escape and a better life. It acts as a motivator that spurs them on to achieve their goals.

Part of Christina's success also came from her persistence. She submitted a demo tape to *Star Search* and later appeared on the show. Although she lost, losing only intensified her desire to keep trying. Christina began singing the National Anthem at professional sports events. She found the large crowds exhilarating. Obviously, Christina was not a person who suffered from stage fright—something that was very important if she wanted to become a star.

Later, she submitted a demo to Disney studios and although she was not accepted at first, Christina did not give up. Eventually, she was invited to join *The All New Mickey Mouse Club*, a popular television show that featured young, talented singers.

This environment helped to develop Christina's talents and also introduced her to other young people just like herself. At school outside of Pittsburgh, Christina had felt out of place—unlike other kids. And they had spurned and bullied her because of her singing abilities. But at Disney where she became part of a large family of like-minded kids, she shone. Here Christina developed more self-confidence and a feeling that her dream was not so unusual, after all.

In that environment, Christina met a woman, Ruth Inniss, who became her talent agent. An agent is essential in helping any artist along the pathway to new opportunities. Without an agent, an aspiring new talent cannot meet producers and recording executives who can help her produce and market new albums.

This one enabled Christina to cut a demo recording. A second agent brought her to the attention of RCA, one of the leading American record labels. Her voice so impressed one of the executives that he had to take notice of her. At RCA, Christina's outsized talent and a unique opportunity had come together to further her career.

Then, almost without warning, Christina found herself at the right place at just the right time. Disney had contacted RCA, looking for someone to sing the theme song of *Mulan,* the studio's new animated film. At this point, Christina showed her own initiative, recorded a similar piece of music, and got the job.

In a sense she had made her own luck—another prerequisite to success. When opportunity struck, she

Talented, determined, and ambitious, Christina was able to transition from child entertainer to pop star to singing legend.

knew how to take advantage of it. This is another trait that is essential to becoming a star.

From there, Christina went on to record "Genie in a Bottle," and "What a Girl Wants." And in 2000, she won the Grammy Award for Best New Artist. *Billboard* also recognized her as the Top Female Pop Act of 2000. At nineteen years old, she had arrived. Christina's goal of becoming a star had been realized.

There is an old saying: "Be Careful What You Wish For." Christina had achieved what she wanted—fame, constant publicity, millions of fans, plenty of money, and prestigious awards that celebrated her abilities. But she could only win the award for "Best New Artist" once. After that, she had to begin setting new goals for herself. And at nineteen, she was being asked to demonstrate a level of maturity that few young women are expected to possess.

At first, she took a few unsteady steps. Christina spoke openly about things that might better have been left unsaid, seemingly unaware of the fact that she would be quoted in the media and might not be fully understood by her fans. Gradually, however, Christina learned to be more guarded.

She also looked around at herself and realized that becoming a pop star was not the only thing she wanted. But when she tried to change the sound of her music and compose her own songs, RCA tried to stop their new singing sensation from becoming too independent. The record company was afraid that if Christina strayed from what her fans liked, RCA might take a huge financial loss.

Christina was upset at not getting her own way. She was already gaining a reputation for being too assertive with her colleagues, and even insensitive to her fans. Some thought that the new star was too self-centered, too focused on her own career to give any thought to anyone else.

But courageously, Christina did not give up. Yes, she was now a star and believed that stardom gave her the freedom to chart a new course—one that might not completely win the approval of RCA. In 2001, she sang the theme song from the major motion picture *Moulin Rouge,* called "Lady Marmalade." This song was a marked departure from her image as a clean-cut teenage pop star. And some of her young fans were stunned.

The following year, Christina released her album *Stripped*, one that continued to take her down the new path that she had charted for herself. One of the songs, "Beautiful," reached number two on the music charts in the United States. And in 2004, Christina was awarded

Christina's Latino Roots

During her career, Christina has been criticized for not emphasizing her Latino roots. But she strong disagrees. "I've dealt with that my whole life. I don't speak the language fluently. And I'm split right down the middle, half Irish and half Ecuadorean. I should not have to prove my ethnicity to anyone. I know who I am. I wouldn't be questioned [about my heritage] if I looked more stereotypically Latina....All I know is no one can tell me I'm not a proud Latina woman...."[1]

a Grammy for Best Female Pop Vocal Performance for the song.

Christina's decision to move in a new direction had proven to be correct. But it took a lot of guts on her part to make it. Meanwhile, she had been writing her own songs—music that came from her own experiences of falling in love and out of love, dealing with critics of her music and her lifestyle, and the difficulties of finding a firm footing for her career.

Buoyed by this success, Christina went to work on a new album, *Back to Basics,* a double album released in 2006. However, this created more controversy at RCA. They didn't want her to do a double album, because it was too big a financial risk. And they didn't entirely support the style of music—much of it with a sound from the 1930s and 1940s—that Christina featured on her new album.

Once again, Christina went ahead. Once again, she achieved success with an album that eventually sold over 4 million copies. And from there she did not look back. There's nothing like success to give an individual an extra boost of confidence in herself.

Even more importantly, Christina had made the decision to do *Back to Basics* because she did not want to lock herself into one style of music. She believed that this might make her a "flash in the pan," with a career that shot up like a meteor and quickly disappeared. She had watched other pop stars who experienced this type of fate. Christina was determined that the same thing would not happen to her.

So Christina kept experimenting, taking risks, and walking a thin line between success and failure. At the end of 2010, bad luck finally caught up with her. She filed for divorce from her husband, Jordan Bratman, starred in a film, *Burlesque,* that was largely panned by the critics, and shortly afterward released her new album *Bionic.*

By any measure, *Bionic* was a failure. It featured a heavy-handed dose of electronic sound effects. These not only disappointed Christina's fans, but the result was an album that sounded like so many others that were being released at the same time. Most importantly, the album did not showcase Christina's magnificent voice— her most important characteristic as a singer.

Christina Quotes

Christina Aguilera has been in show business for so long, she has experienced it all. She also has not been shy in expressing her feelings to the press. Here are just a few of her quotes:

"For me, my voice and music was always an outlet. Growing up in an unstable environment. . .music was my only real escape." *Rolling Stone*, August 24, 2006[2]

"I think an artist can fit under a few different categories depending on how much you explore your creativity. . . .I thrive on creativity. So in the long run I want to be an all-around entertainer." *MSN Live*, 2000[3]

"If you are a woman and you're assertive and you want to get the job done, you're a b. . . .If you're a guy, you're just assertive." *Glamour Magazine*, January 2007[4]

Thanks to her desire to grow and change as an artist, Christina has a long career ahead of her. Her fans look forward to following her.

All these experiences taught Christina that her life was not one magical moment after another. And now she would find out whether she had the courage to bounce back.

Once again, the answer was a resounding yes! Christina went back to the drawing board and released *Lotus*. And like a lotus, she emerged from failure with an album that brought her near the top of the charts. She continued touring across the world. Sometimes the pace was grueling, because every star must not only produce new material but appear in front of their fans continually. It's the only way to keep their names in front of the public, receive publicity, and stay at the top.

Christina followed these successes with a permanent role in *The Voice* that was praised by television critics. She not only gave the show a tremendous boost, but also boosted her own career.

Perhaps the best indication of how successful a star can be is how many times she can reinvent herself...how many times she can deal with failure and bounce back... how long she can stay at the top. As time goes on, and she is no longer a fresh, new face, the task grows even harder.

Christina managed to master all the elements necessary for a long career—one that would constantly reintroduce her with new music to generations of music fans. By these measures, Christina Aguilera has shown herself a shining star.

Chronology

1980—Christina Aguilera is born in Staten Island, New York.

1986—Christina's sister is born.
Shelly Aguilera leaves her husband.

1990—Appears on *Star Search*.

1992—Joins the cast of *The All New Mickey Mouse Club*.
Christina's mother, Shelly, remarries.

1994—Ruth Inniss becomes Christina's agent.
The All New Mickey Mouse Club is cancelled.

1995—Records a demo album, *Just Be Free*.

1999—"Reflection" becomes a number one hit in America.
Christina releases "Genie in a Bottle."
Releases her first album, *Christina Aguilera*.

2000—Appears in the Super Bowl half-time show.
Begins first headlining tour.
Releases *Mi Reflejo* (My Reflection) album.
Releases *My Kind of Christmas* album.
Wins a Grammy Award for Best New Artist.
Billboard calls Aguilera the Top Female Pop Act of 2000.

2001—Performs "Lady Marmalade" in *Moulin Rouge* movie.
Receives awards at the *Billboard* Latin Music Awards.

2002—*Stripped* reaches the top ranks of *Billboard* 200.
Wins a Grammy for "Lady Marmalade."

2003—Named Top Female Pop Act of 2003 by *Billboard*.

2004—Wins a Grammy Award for Best Female Pop Vocal Performance for "Beautiful."

2005—Marries Jordan Bratman.

2006—Releases *Back to Basics* album.

2007—Wins a Grammy Award for "Ain't No Other Man."
Joins "End Violence Against Women" campaign.

2008—Gives birth to a son, Max.
Releases "Keeps Gettin' Better."

2010—*Bionic,* Christina's new album, is released.
Stars in *Burlesque* with Cher.
Becomes an ambassador for the United Nations
(UN) World Food Program (WFP).

2011—Divorces Jordan Bratman.
Begins appearing as a coach on *The Voice.*

2012—Releases new album, *Lotus.*

2014—Engaged to Matt Rutler.
Daughter, Summer Rain, is born.

2015—Returns to *The Voice.*
Appears at the Academy of Country Music
Awards.
Wins a Grammy Award for Best Pop Duo/Group
Performance.

Chapter Notes

CHAPTER 1. A CHILD STAR

1. "Star Search Losers Who Made It Big," ABC News, November 28, 2001, http://abcnews.go.com/2020/story?id=123814&page=1.
2. Neill Straus, "Christina Aguilera: The Hit Girl," *Rolling Stone,* July 6, 2000.

CHAPTER 2. A YOUNG SINGING SENSATION

1. Pier Dominguez, *A Star Is Made* (Phoenix: Colossus Books, 2003), p. 3.
2. Chloe Govan, *Christina Aguilera* (London, England: Omnibus Press, 2013), p. 6.
3. Ibid., p. 8.
4. Ibid., p. 12.
5. Dominguez, p. 9.
6. Govan, p. 13.
7. Dominguez, p. 17.

CHAPTER 3. CHRISTINA'S GROWING FAMILY

1. Chloe Govan, *Christina Aguilera* (London, England: Omnibus Press, 2013), p. 17.
2. Neil Strauss, "Christina Aguilera: The Hit Girl," *Rolling Stone,* July 6, 2000.
3. Rebecca Sodergren, "The Right Note," *Pittsburgh Post-Gazette,* July 30, 1998, 47.
4. Govan, p. 21.
5. Strauss, "Christina Aguilera: The Hit Girl."
6. Ibid.

CHAPTER 4. TEEN POP STAR

1. Richard Harrington, "Christina Aguilera: No Mickey Mouse Pop Sensation," *The Washington Post,* September 8, 1999, C1.
2. Pier Dominguez, *A Star Is Made* (Phoenix: Colossus Books, 2003), pp. 69–73.
3. Sophfronia Scott Gregory, "Uncorking the Genie," *People.Com,* September 27, 1999, http://www.people.com/people/article/0,,20129327,00.html.
4. Richard Harrington, "Christina Aguilera's Fast Track: Ex-Mouseketeer Has the Voice to Pull Away from Teenpop Pack," *The Washington Post,* February 13, 2000, G1.
5. Gregory, "Uncorking the Genie."
6. Dominguez, p. 97.
7. Neil Strauss, "Cristina Aguilera: The Hit Girl," *Rolling Stone,* July 6, 2000.
8. Ibid.

CHAPTER 5. LOVE AND SUCCESS

1. Pier Dominguez, *A Star Is Made* (Phoenix: Colossus Books), 2003, p. 137.
2. Chloe Govan, *Christina Aguilera* (London, England: Omnibus Press, 2013), p. 56.
3. Ibid., p. 75.
4. Ibid., p. 70.
5. Ed Masley, "An Outrageously Adult Aguilera Kicks Off Her First Headlining Tour," July 13, 2000, *Pittsburgh Post-Gazette,* D1.
6. Ed Masley, "Aguilera Wows 'Em With Awesome Vocals," *Pittsburgh Post-Gazette,* August 28, 2000, A6.

CHAPTER 6. MOVING ON

1. "Christina Aguilera," *Allure Magazine,* April 16, 2002.
2. Ed Masley, "Concert Review: Aguilera Wows 'Em with Awe-Inspiring Vocals," *Pittsburgh Post-Dispatch,* August 27, 2000.
3. Pier Dominguez, *A Star Is Made* (Phoenix: Colossus Books, 2003), pp. 198–200.
4. Ed Masley, "An Outrageously Adult Aguilera Kicks Off Her First Headlining Tour," July 13, 2000, *Pittsburgh Post-Gazette*, D1.
5. Kelefa Sanneh, "The New Season/Music; Idol Returns, Her Image Remade," *The New York Times,* September 8, 2002

CHAPTER 7. A NEW IMAGE

1. Elysa Gardner, "Aguilera's Image Is Stripped," *USA Today,* October 24, 2002, http://usatoday30. usatoday.com/life/music/news/2002-10-23-christina-aguilera_x.htm.
2. Kelefa Sanneh, "The New Season/Music; Idol Returns, Her Image Remade," *The New York Times,* September 8, 2002.
3. Ibid.
4. Nick Duerden, "The Good, the Bad and the Dirty," *Blender,* December 2003, http://www. christinamultimedia.com/newssource/index. phparticleID=2949.

CHAPTER 8. CHRISTINA AND BRITNEY

1. Chloe Govan, *Christina Aguilera* (London, England: Omnibus Press, 2013), pp. 139–140.

2. Sam Lansky, "Britney Spears' Shotgun Wedding Turns 10: Remember 55 Magical Hours," *Rolling Stone,* January 3, 2014.

CHAPTER 9. GIVING BACK

1. "Domestic Violence Statistics," http://domesticviolencestatistics.org/domestic-violence-statistics/.
2. "Aguilera Plans Shelter for Domestic Abuse Victims," July 29, 2006, http://www.femalefirst.co.uk/celebrity/Christina+Aguilera-10955.html.
3. Ibid.
4. "Aguilera Highlights Domestic Abuse on Army Bases," WENN, August 7, 2006, http://www.contactmusic.com/christina-aguilera/news/aguilera-highlights-domestic-violence-on-army-bases.
5. Ibid.
6. Alan Cole, "Christina Aguilera: Humanitarian Award," *Charity News,* May 10, 2012, http://www.giving-news.com/news/1769/christina-aguilera-humanitarian-award.html.
7. "How Christina Aguilera Gives Back," *Redbook,* http://www.redbookmag.com/life/charity/interviews/g869/christina-aguilera-helps-hungry-children/.
8. Ibid.

CHAPTER 10. BACK TO BASICS

1. Kelefa Sanneh, "Honey They've Shrunk the Pop Stars (but Christina Aguilera Fights On)," *The New York Times,* August 17, 2006. http://www.nytimes.com/2006/08/17/arts/music/17sann.html?pagewanted=print.

2. Chloe Govan, *Christina Aguilera* (London, England: Omnibus Press, 2013), p. 176.

CHAPTER 11. THE NEXT STAGE

1. Kelefa Sanneh, "Dirrty Girl, Sometimes It's Hard to Be a Woman," *The New York Times,* March 26, 2007, http://www.nytimes.com/2007/03/26/arts/music/26xtin.html?_r=0&pagewanted=print.
2. Ibid.
3. Brian Orloff and Mike Fleeman, "Paris Hilton Makes a Baby Announcement—for Christina Aguilera," *People,* September 9, 2007. http://www.people.com/people/package/article/0,,20053775_20055465,00.html.
4. Scott Mervis,"Music Review," *Pittsburgh Post Gazette,* April 16, 2007, B1, B4.
5. "Christina Aguilera and Jordan Bratman Welcome Max Liron," *People,* January 13, 2008, http://celebrity babies.people.com/2008/01/13/christina-agu-3-4/.
6. Mike Isaac, "The Tiny Moving Message," *New York Times,* August 4, 2015, B1.

CHAPTER 12. SLIDING DOWNHILL

1. Chloe Govan, *Christina Aguilera* (London, England: Omnibus Press, 2013), p. 214.
2. Ibid., p. 218.
3. Ulrica Wihlborg, "Christina Aguilera: Why I Filed for Divorce," *People,* December 2, 2010, http://www.people.com/people/article/0,,20446427,00.html.
4. "Christina Aguilera," *Marie Claire,* February 2012.
5. Rebecca Murray, "Christina Aguilera Talks About 'Burlesque,'" *Movies About.Com,* 2010, http://movies.about.com/od/burlesque/a/Christina-Aguilera-Burlesque.htm.

6. Ibid.

7. Rebecca Murray, "'Burlesque' Movie Review," *Movies About.Com,* http://movies.about.com/od/burlesque/ fr/Burlesque-Movie-Review.htm.

CHAPTER 13. *THE VOICE*

1. Jon Caramanica, "Be a Star, Then You Can Judge," *The New York Times,* September 17, 2012, http://www. nytimes.com/2012/09/18/arts/music/how-christina-aguilera-changed-judging-of-reality-....

2. "Christina Aguilera Biography," *People.Com,* 2014, http://www.people.com/people/christina_aguilera/ biography/0,,20004434_20,00.html.

3. "The Voice, The Live Finale, Part 2," http://www. nbc.com/the-voice/episode-guide/season-8/the-live-finale-part-2/828.

4. "Christina Aguilera's Colorful Hair and Makeup: All the Details!," *Us Weekly,* 2015, http://www. usmagazine.com/celebrity-beauty/news/christina-aguileras-colorful-hair-and-makeup.

5. "Christina Aguilera Talks Childhood Pain, Divorce, Superbowl Screwup, 'Burlesque' Failure in W Magazine," *Huffington Post,* June 15, 2011, http:// www.huffingtonpost.com/2011/06/15/christina-aguilera-divorce-superbowl-jeremy-re....

6. Ibid.

7. Elizabeth A. Harris, "Singing, Aguilera Trips O'er Ramparts," *The New York Times,* February 6, 2011, http://www.nytimes.com/2011/02/07/sports/ football/07aguilera-super-bowl-pregame.html.

8. Ibid.

CHAPTER 14. *LOTUS*

1. "Christina Aguilera Biography," *People.Com,* 2014, http://www.people.com/people/christina_aguilera/ biography/0,,20004434_20,00.html.
2. Mesfin Fekadu, "Christina Aguilera, 'Lotus' Review: Good, But Not Great," *Huffington Post,* November 12, 2012, http://www.huffingtonpost.com/2012/11/12/ christina-aguilera-lotus-review_n_2119130.html.
3. "Christina Aguilera Biography."
4. Elizabeth Messina, "Christina Aguilera, New Baby, New Life," *People,* 2/11/2015, http://celebritybabies. people.com/2015/02/11/christina-aguilera-daughter-summer-rain-first-...
5. Ibid.

CHAPTER 15. THE FUTURE OF A SINGING SENSATION

1. Julianne Ishler, "Christina Aguilera Mocks Britney Spears & More in Hysterical Video," *Hollywood Life,* May 19, 2015, http://hollywoodlife.com/2015/05/19/ christina-aguilera-mocks-celebrities-britney-spears-the....
2. Rachel McRady, "Christina Aguilera Goes Brunette for Nashville: See Her Dramatic New Hair Color Pic!" *US Weekly,* March 17, 2015, http://www.usmagazine.com/ celebrity-beauty/news/christina-aguilera-brunette-nashville-hai...
3. "Christina Aguilera Perfumes: Awards Won," 2014, http://www.perfulmes.christinaaguilara.com/en/ awards.
4. "Christina Aguilera's Clothing Line," *Daily Makeover,* February 9, 2011.

5. "Christina Aguilera Steals the Show During NBA All-Star Game," *Latin Times,* February 15, 2015, http://www.latintimes.com/pulse/Christina-aguilera-steals-show-during-nba-all-star-game-29. . . .

CHAPTER 16. THE ELEMENTS OF SUCCESS

1. "Christina Aguilera Addresses 'Not Latina Enough' Criticism, Opens Up About Her Hispanic Heritage and Estranged Father," *Huffington Post,* February 7, 2012, http://www.huffingtonpost.com/2012/02/07/christina-aguileraaguilera-_n_1258067.html.

2. Austin Scaggs, "Christina Aguilera: Dirty Girl Cleans Up," *Rolling Stone,* August 24, 2006, http://www.rollingstone.com/music/features/dirty-girl-cleans-up-20060824.

3. Christina Aguilera, MSNLive Chat, June 8, 2000, http://www.bignoisenow.com/christina/msn.html

4. "Christina Aguilera Quotes," 2015, http://www.notable-quotes.com/a/aguilera_christina.html.

Glossary

Billboard magazine—A publication that charts top releases in the music industry.

camp—A style based on deliberate theatricality.

demo album—A musical artist's audition tape.

diva—The star of a show.

electronica—Electronic enhancements that give an almost digital sound.

gold record—A recording that sells one hundred thousand copies.

Grammy Award—Most prestigious annual awards for music stars.

lip-synch—When a singer mouths the words while a recording plays the song.

platinum record—A recording that sells one million copies.

pop music—A version of rock and roll that comes from the term "popular" music.

R&B—Rhythm and Blues' style music.

rap—A style of music in which rhymed lines are sung to a heavy beat.

talent agent—A person who helps a professional entertainer obtain jobs and negotiates payments for performances.

tour—When a singer travels to different locations to perform songs for live audiences.

Further Reading

BOOKS

Dominguez, Pier. *Christina Aguilera: A Star Is Made.* Phoenix: Colossus Books, 2011.

Donovan, Mary Anne. *Christina Aguilera: A Biography.* Santa Barbara, CA: Greenwood, 2010.

Govan, Chloe. *Christina Aguilera.* London, England: Omnibus Press, 2013.

WEBSITES

Billboard

www.billboard.com/charts

The website for Billboard magazine shows up-to-the-minute chart positions for a variety of genres of music.

The Official Christina Aguilera Site

www.christinaaguilera.com

Christina Aguilera's official website

The Voice

www.nbc.com/the-voice

Official website for NBC's The Voice.

MOVIES

Burlesque. Directed by Steve Antin, 2010.

Moulin Rouge. Directed by Baz Luhrmann, 2001.

Index